The Making of the United Kingdom 1500-1750

Unification

Nathaniel Harris

WAYLAND

The Making of the United Kingdom 1500-1750

Church and People
Crown and Parliament
Social Change
Unification

Cover: Queen Anne receiving the Treaty of Union in 1707; (inset) Women and children flee from English troops during fierce fighting at the Battle of Culloden, 1746.

Series and Book Editor: Rosemary Ashley
Designer: Joyce Chester

First published in 1996 by Wayland Publishers Ltd, 61 Western Road, Hove, East Sussex, BN3 1JD, England

British Library Cataloguing in Publication Data

Harris, Nathaniel, 1937–
   Unification. – (The making of the United Kingdom, 1500–1750)
   1. Great Britain – History – Modern period, 1485– – Juvenile literature
   I. Title
   941'.05

   ISBN 0 7502 1815 0

Typeset by Joyce Chester
Printed and bound in Italy by G. Canale & C.S.p.A., Turin

Picture acknowledgements
The pictures in this book were supplied by: AKG London 12, 25 (lower), 27; Bridgeman Art Library /Belvoir Castle 15, /British Library 42 (lower), /Crown Estates – Institute of Directors 40, /Imperial Defence College 35, /King Street Galleries 41 (lower), /Private Collection 28 (lower), /Royal Society of Arts 11; C. M. Dixon 43; Mary Evans Picture Library 5, 9 (lower), 10, 14, 22, 25 (top), 31, 37; Eye Ubiquitous /James Davis 9 (top), /Tony Brown 44; Hulton Deutsch 8, 16, 17, 18, 20, 26, 28 (top), 29 (both), 30, 36, 41 (top); National Gallery of Scotland cover (main picture), 39; National Portrait Gallery 7, 23, 32, 38; National Trust of Scotland 24, 34, 42 (inset); Wayland Picture Library 33 (both). Maps on pages 4, 13, 19 are by Peter Bull Design.

Contents

1

Divided Islands

The British Isles are a small group of neighbouring islands just off the mainland of Europe. By 1500 the two main islands, which we now call Britain and Ireland, had been inhabited for almost a thousand years by four different peoples, each with its own strong sense of identity.

A map showing the British Isles in about 1500. Control of Wales is divided between the Crown and the Marcher lords. In Ireland, English rule is only effective in the Pale, the area around Dublin. Scotland is an entirely independent kingdom.

The Pale c.1500

Crown Lands in Wales

Marcher lordships

ORKNEY ISLES

SHETLAND ISLES

SCOTLAND

Edinburgh

IRELAND

Dublin

ENGLAND

York

WALES

Carmarthen

Bosworth

London

The English Parliament meeting during the reign of Henry VIII. The King is shown dominating the proceedings. However, the crucial role taken by Parliament in Henry's policy-making meant that it became much more important in the government of the country.

The English, Welsh, Scots and Irish had separate traditions and distinctive national symbols and patron saints. Perhaps most important of all, they had their own national heroes, who were felt to sum up the spirit of the nation – heroes such as Ireland's Brian Boru, killed in the hour of victory over the Vikings at Clontarf (1014) and Robert Bruce, King of Scotland, whose army slaughtered the English at Bannockburn (1314).

The Island Peoples

History and geography worked together to create four different peoples in the British Isles. 'Britain' was the Roman name for the largest island. Both Britain and Ireland were inhabited by Celts until the Angles and Saxons (or Anglo-Saxons) began to invade and settle from the fifth century. The area eventually occupied by the Anglo-Saxons came to be called Angle-Land, or England. But the Anglo-Saxons failed to conquer the more rugged, distant lands to the west and north – Wales and Scotland – and they never crossed over to Ireland. So Wales, Scotland and Ireland developed differently from England and, in time, from one another.

After centuries of invasions, battles and treaties, these island peoples were far from united. England had been organized as a strong state after the Norman Conquest of 1066, and had begun to expand. But most English kings were more interested in trying to hold on to parts of France than in conquering their British neighbours. By 1500 the English royal family and their barons ruled all of Wales. But they had only a foothold in Ireland, while the Scots remained completely independent and, allied to the French, were always a threat to English security.

Yet in little more than two centuries after 1500, mainland Britain became a single state. England, Wales and Scotland all recognized the authority of one Crown and sent MPs to the parliament at Westminster. Ireland was also brought firmly under the control of the Crown, although serious discontent and conflict went on unresolved for centuries. The British Crown and Parliament effectively ruled the entire British Isles. As a unified country, governed from London, by the 1750s Britain was able to become a great imperial and trading power.

This book explains how these great changes came about. They were largely unplanned and to some extent accidental. The upheavals of the late-fifteenth, sixteenth and seventeenth centuries (see diagram below) all had an influence on how and when the different parts of Britain came together. The union between England and Wales took place in the 1530s, as part of a strengthening and centralization of government under Henry VIII. Ireland was subdued by force at the end of Queen Elizabeth I's reign (1558–1603), after Spanish landings in Ireland had shown how important it was for England to control the next-door island.

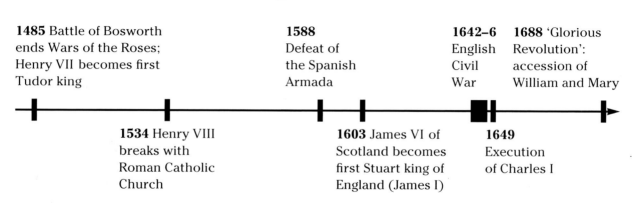

1485 Battle of Bosworth ends Wars of the Roses; Henry VII becomes first Tudor king

1588 Defeat of the Spanish Armada

1642–6 English Civil War

1688 'Glorious Revolution': accession of William and Mary

1534 Henry VIII breaks with Roman Catholic Church

1603 James VI of Scotland becomes first Stuart king of England (James I)

1649 Execution of Charles I

Charles I, whose disastrous reign (1625–49) ended with his execution. At that time, with civil war in England, wars between England and Scotland and rebellion in Ireland, unification seemed very unlikely.

The traditional enemies, England and Scotland, became a little closer by taking the same side – the Protestant side – in the religious conflicts that were tearing Europe apart in the sixteenth century. Most important of all, in 1603 the King of Scotland, James VI, also succeeded to the English throne, as James I.

But although they had the same king, England and Scotland remained separate countries all through the seventeenth century. Sometimes their interests clashed, for example when Scottish armies joined in the English Civil War on the side of Parliament, and when the English parliamentary leader, Oliver Cromwell, invaded and conquered Scotland. It was another fifty years before the two countries willingly agreed to the Act of Union (1707) which joined England, Wales and Scotland into a single country, known as Great Britain.

2

England and Wales

Edward I (1239–1307) was famous during his lifetime as a crusader, lawmaker and conqueror. Having subdued Wales, he went on to become the 'Hammer of the Scots'.

From the time of the Norman Conquest of England in 1066 the Welsh were hard-pressed to keep their independence. The Normans were formidable foes, with their heavy armour and their strong, well-fortified castles. They managed to occupy some parts of Wales, but the Welsh fought back fiercely. The Normans conquered quite a lot of the south and part of the north-east, but most of the country was still ruled by Welsh princes.

The Norman invaders were not members of their king's army but great lords who had been granted lands along the English border with Wales. William I (the Conqueror) gave them the lands so that they would guard the borders against Welsh attacks. These border lands were known as Marches, and the lords were called Marcher lords. The lords owed a basic loyalty to the king, but they had special rights and their own territories, and English law was not in force there. In practice, the Marcher lords often behaved as if they were independent rulers, sometimes fighting each other as well as the Welsh.

For much of the time the Welsh were divided, serving a number of different princes. But in the thirteenth century Llywelyn ap Gruffud became the overlord of other Welsh rulers, and was recognized as Prince of Wales by the English king Henry III. Then Henry's successor, Edward I, quarrelled with Llywelyn and invaded Wales. Edward, a great warrior-king, fought two wars against the Welsh, which ended when Llywelyn was killed in 1282. To hold down the Welsh, Edward built a mighty chain of castles, such as Caernarfon, Conwy and Beaumaris, which are still magnificent sights today. After a last great revolt in 1294 the Welsh seemed to accept defeat. In 1301 Edward named his son as the new Prince of Wales. From this time onwards the oldest son of the king or queen usually became Prince of

Wales – a tradition that is kept up to this day. (Charles, the eldest son of Queen Elizabeth II, is the present Prince of Wales.)

Conwy Castle in North Wales, one of a chain of castles built by Edward I to hold down the Welsh.

Many Welsh people hated English rule so much that they broke out in a great national revolt, led by Owain Glyn Dŵr (c.1354–c.1415). Owain used this hatred to help his cause, writing to a powerful supporter:

The Welsh leader Owain Glyn Dŵr, Prince of Wales.

> '*We inform you that we hope to be able, by God's help and yours, to deliver the Welsh people from captivity of our English enemies, who, for a long time ... have oppressed us and our ancestors.*'

When the revolt was defeated, the Welsh found themselves even worse off than before, because an angry English parliament passed harsh laws against them. They could not hold meetings, become government officials, carry weapons, or live in a fortified town. The laws were not always enforced (especially if a Welshman was wealthy and had powerful friends), but they clearly showed that the English regarded the Welsh as an inferior people.

The Son of Prophecy?

Owain Glyn Dŵr (c.1354–c.1415) was a wealthy squire, said to be descended from the ancient royal families of Wales. In 1400 he led a revolt against Henry IV of England. Owain was widely believed to have magic powers, and to be the long-awaited 'son of prophecy' who would liberate the Welsh from English rule. He was proclaimed Prince of Wales, held a Welsh parliament, and formed an alliance with English rebels and the French king, who sent troops to help him. But although he was successful at first, from 1405 the English reconquered Wales. Owain waged guerrilla warfare against them until 1413, but nothing more is known about him after that.

Later in the fifteenth century, the Wars of the Roses divided the English into rival groups, the Lancastrians and the Yorkists, who fought each other for the English crown. Welshmen too fought on both sides. But by 1485 the Lancastrian leader was Henry Tudor, Earl of Richmond, who had been born and brought up in Wales. After years in exile he returned, determined to overthrow the Yorkist king Richard III. He landed at Milford Haven, in the south-west of the country, and claimed to be the rightful Prince of Wales. He told the Welsh people that he was freeing them from their slave-like state – 'delivering them of such miserable servitudes as they have piteously stood in'. He also flew a flag with the red dragon of Wales on it. Then he marched across Wales to do battle with Richard III.

Of course, Henry Tudor appealed to other groups as well as the Welsh. But Welsh support probably made the difference between victory and defeat at the battle of Bosworth on 22 August 1485 – about a third of Henry's army were Welshmen. Richard was killed in the battle, and Henry Tudor became King Henry VII.

The Earl of Richmond's forces advance at the Battle of Bosworth in 1485. Richmond's victory ended the Wars of the Roses and he became Henry VII, the first of the Tudor monarchs.

A Welsh King for England

Owain ap Tudor (c.1400–1461) was a Welsh squire at the English court. Queen Katherine, the widow of Henry V, fell in love with him and they were secretly married. Eventually their marriage became accepted and their sons, Edmund and Jasper, were made Earls of Richmond and Pembroke. Edmund married Katherine Beaufort, a descendant of Edward III. Their son, Henry Tudor (1457–1509), was Welsh through his father and grandfather. Later he was able to claim the throne through his mother, so the Welsh squire's grandson became king of England in 1485.

Henry VII, an English king with strong Welsh ties.

Henry was the first monarch of the Tudor dynasty, which ruled England until 1603. The Welsh found it easier to accept a king of England who seemed to be like one of themselves. Clever Welshmen could now make careers at the English court, and many of the anti-Welsh laws were eased. However, Wales and England remained separate countries.

Over the next few years the power of the Crown grew steadily greater in Wales and many Marcher lordships were taken over by the king. But the really important change – a full union of England and Wales – occurred in 1536, during the reign of Henry VIII (1509–47). Henry's chief minister, Thomas Cromwell, certainly wanted to create a strong English state. This was happening in other European countries such as France and Spain, so England needed to keep pace. But the most pressing reason was that Henry had just carried through a revolution – the English Reformation. This made the King head of the Church instead of the Pope. Many other changes were involved, affecting people's everyday lives, and King Henry needed to keep the tightest possible control over his subjects.

So Parliament passed the 'Act for Laws and Justice to be Ministered in Wales in like form as it is in this Realm'. The most important statements in the Act were that:

11

Thomas Cromwell (c.1485–1540) was Chancellor of the Exchequer and chief adviser to Henry VIII.

> *'His highness hath by the advice, agreement and authority of Parliament established that his country of Wales shall be from henceforth united with this realm of England.'*

and that:

> *'All persons born in Wales shall have, enjoy and inherit all the freedoms, liberties, rights, privileges and laws within the realm.'*

In other words, England and Wales became one country under the Crown, with the Welsh as full citizens. The Marcher lordships disappeared, and Wales was divided into shires, just as in England. The Welsh counties and boroughs sent MPs to Parliament at Westminster. English laws and rules about inheriting property now applied to Wales. Welshmen could hold any office – but all government and legal business had to be carried out in the English language.

Since England was larger and wealthier than Wales, the change opened up many opportunities for Welsh people. On the other hand, English became the official language and Welsh traditions suffered. For the wealthy, well-born and educated Welsh, the union was exactly what they wanted. By the 1590s a Welsh historian was claiming that:

> *'No country in England so flourisheth in one hundred years as Wales has done, since the government of Henry VII to this time.'*

3

The Conquest of Ireland

Ireland lies at the very edge of Europe, separated from the continent by the sea and by its British neighbour. For long periods of its history, Ireland has been relatively isolated. The Romans, who conquered Britain, never landed in Ireland, but Roman goods and influences did reach the country. Christianity arrived in the fifth century, after which the Irish Church produced many great scholars and missionaries.

Ireland remained a Celtic society with its own laws and customs. The economy was pastoral (based on herding animals rather than growing crops). The country was divided into rival clans and small, short-lived kingdoms.

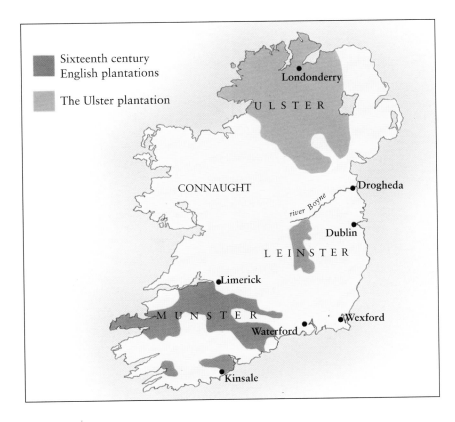

Sixteenth century
English plantations

The Ulster plantation

Londonderry

ULSTER

CONNAUGHT

Drogheda

river Boyne

Dublin

LEINSTER

Limerick

MUNSTER

Wexford

Waterford

Kinsale

A map of Ireland showing the most important places mentioned in this book. The coloured areas represent the 'plantations' under Elizabeth I and James I/VI (see pages 16 and 27).

English forces confront an Irish clan chief and his warriors in 1294, when Richard II was campaigning in Ireland.

Like many parts of Europe, Ireland suffered terribly from Viking raids. However, in the ninth century the Vikings founded the first Irish towns – Dublin, Wexford and Waterford – which traded with the outside world.

Like Wales, Ireland was invaded from Britain by the Normans. In 1166 Desmond, one of the Irish kings, asked a powerful Norman lord, the Earl of Pembroke, to help him regain his throne. Pembroke, nicknamed 'Strongbow', was so successful that after Desmond's death he took over his kingdom of Leinster. Other Norman barons soon began to carve out great Irish lordships for themselves. In 1171 the king of England, Henry II, arrived with a large army, not to conquer Ireland but to make sure that Strongbow and other Norman lords accepted his authority as 'Lord of Ireland'.

Over the next century, more adventurers and traders crossed to Ireland, pushing back the native Irish people.

14

By 1300 two-thirds of Ireland was ruled or colonized by the Normans – or rather the English, since the Normans and Saxons had by this time merged into one people. Royal officials governed from Dublin and an Irish parliament developed. The English attitude to the native Irish was expressed by the writer Gerald of Wales (1146–1223):

> *'Dedicated only to leisure and laziness, this is a truly barbarous people. They depend for their livelihood on animals and they live like animals.'*

After 1300 colonization ground to a halt. Ireland became divided between the Gaelic-speaking Irish in the north and west, and the descendants of the Norman colonists, known as the Anglo-Irish. The English kings lost much of their power in Ireland, and by 1500 the Lord Deputy, the governor appointed by the king, controlled only a small coastal area around Dublin known as the Pale.

When Henry VII became king in 1485, the Lord Deputy was the powerful Earl of Kildare. Even though the earl had backed the wrong (Yorkist) side in the Wars of the Roses (see page 10), Henry had to keep him as Lord Deputy. When he tried to replace the earl, Kildare was able to cause so much trouble that the king had to reappoint him.

The only alternative would have been for Henry to gather a large army and make a proper conquest of Ireland. But that would have cost too much money and time, for English monarchs were usually more concerned about security at home, fighting the Scots and affairs in Europe. As long as Ireland was not a threat to England – for example as a base for a rival power – English kings preferred to spend as little on the country as possible and keep things much as they were. This was even true of the masterful Henry VIII. In 1515 more than sixty regions in Ireland were reported to be:

> *'...inhabited with the King's enemies ... where reigneth more than sixty chief captains ... and every one of them maketh war and peace for himself without any licence of the King.'*

But there were some important changes during Henry's reign. In 1534 the King was finally able to get rid of the Earl of Kildare when he mercilessly crushed a rebellion by the

Henry VIII (1491–1547) was one of the most ruthless of English monarchs. He defied the Pope and greatly strengthened the Crown. In 1541 he took the title 'King of Ireland', but the Irish remained rebellious and unruly.

This print shows Irish clan warfare in the sixteenth century. Although they were fierce fighters, the Irish were poorly equipped by comparison with their English rulers, and they could not hope to defeat an English army in open battle.

Irish leader. From now on the Lord Deputy would at least be a man chosen for his loyalty to the King. Finally, in 1541, Henry took the title of King of Ireland.

There was no longer any doubt about who was supposed to rule Ireland. But real control was hard to achieve, and became harder still when bitter religious conflicts developed. Under Elizabeth I (r. 1558–1603), England became a Protestant country, violently opposed to Roman Catholicism. But in Ireland the great majority of the Irish and the 'Old English' (Anglo-Irish) remained Catholics.

Catholic Spain was the most powerful nation in Europe and was increasingly hostile to England. This meant that Catholic Ireland was a weak point in England's defences, likely to rebel and welcome help from Spain. As one lord deputy wrote to Elizabeth, this might be 'such a ruin to England as I am afeard to think on'.

Elizabeth was cautious and unwilling to spend money. But events forced her to become active in Ireland. An Irish rebellion in 1579–83 was backed by landings of Italian and Spanish soldiers. The Queen had to send a large force, which only defeated the rebels and invaders after savage fighting. Munster was laid waste and a 'plantation' was begun – that is, a colony of Protestant English settlers were 'planted' on lands taken from the rebels. The idea was to establish a loyal colony to help hold down hostile territory. The new arrivals formed a group very different from the long-settled Old English, who had remained Catholic. Bound together by religion, the Old English and Irish gradually merged into a single group.

During Elizabeth's reign, English law and government slowly extended over much of Ireland. The main exception was the large northern province of Ulster, still inhabited by Gaelic-speaking Irish and ruled by the clan chief Hugh O'Neill. He had an up-to-date knowledge of warfare and had carefully built up an efficient army, much stronger than anything that other Irish lords had been able to raise.

O'Neill may not have wanted to rebel, but the strengthening of English rule threatened his position, and a series of disputes led to fighting. O'Neill's great victory at the Yellow Ford (1598) encouraged rebellion in other parts of Ireland, and because he was so powerful, Elizabeth had to act decisively. She sent a large army, led by her favourite, the Earl of Essex, against O'Neill. Essex achieved little, but in 1600 his successor, Lord Mountjoy, found the right plan. Mountjoy whittled away O'Neill's resources, strengthening English garrisons, destroying crops and cattle, and cutting lines of communication.

Hugh O'Neill, Earl of Tyrone [c. 1550–1616]

O'Neill was the last of the great Irish chiefs to rule independently. Although he was Earl of Tyrone, his real power was based on his position as 'the O'Neill', the clan chief. The strengthening of English rule brought him into conflict with Elizabeth I, and after a long struggle lasting from 1594 to 1603, O'Neill was forced to submit. The old Irish way of life was dead, although the Gaelic language survived. O'Neill fled from Ireland in 1607 and eventually died in exile.

O'Neill's desire to rule all Ulster brought about war with Queen Elizabeth I.

Fierce fighting between English and Irish forces at one of the many battles which took place in Ireland during the sixteenth century.

The ruthless nature of Mountjoy's campaign in Ireland was reported by one of his generals, Sir Arthur Chichester:

'We have killed, burned and spoiled all along the lough [lake] ... We spare none of what quality [rank] or sex soever, and it hath bred much terror in the people.'

O'Neill hoped for help from the Spanish. But when they finally came in 1601, they landed in the south, at Kinsale. O'Neill was forced to leave his base in Ulster and march to meet his allies, but he was defeated on the way and the besieged Spaniards were forced to surrender. The English had conquered Ireland at last.

Warfare in Ireland

Fighting in Ireland was very hard for English troops because of the wet weather and difficult terrain. But they did have great advantages in weapons and organization – until Hugh O'Neill began to train his men in the use of muskets and pikes. The English cavalry was still superior, but O'Neill waged a hit-and-run guerrilla war, darting out of bogs or woodlands and striking at unexpected moments. Although he was successful in the 1590s, O'Neill was beaten when Lord Mountjoy began to wear down Irish resistance.

4

Scotland Defiant

The English conquest of Wales and Ireland was helped by the fact that both of these countries were usually divided between rival chiefs or princes. By contrast, Scotland became a single kingdom at an early date. Even more important was the fact that, although Scots often quarrelled among themselves, they developed a strong national feeling. In a crisis they were able to act together, and they were never permanently conquered.

A map of Scotland showing the main places mentioned in this book, including battles fought against the English during the sixteenth and seventeenth centuries and Jacobite rebellions of the eighteenth century (see chapters 6 and 7).

*William Wallace
(c. 1270–1305) was a
Scottish knight who led his
troops against Edward I of
England (see page 8). He
won a great victory at
Stirling Bridge (1297) but
was defeated the following
year at Falkirk. Eventually
he was captured by the
English and hanged, drawn
and quartered (a favourite
form of execution).*

Yet Scotland was made up of many peoples. In Roman times, the Picts held the far north. Then, about AD 500, the Scots crossed from their home in the north of Ireland and established themselves in Argyll, in the west of the country. In the ninth century the Scots conquered and merged with the Picts. Vikings and Angles also settled among the Scots.

By 1066, when the Normans conquered England, Scotland was a well-established kingdom stretching about as far south as its present-day borders. But for centuries the islands off the northern coasts of Scotland were ruled by Norway – the Western Isles until 1266, and the Orkney and Shetland islands until as late as 1469.

The Scottish kings recognized the military skills of the Normans, and actually encouraged Norman lords and knights to settle in the south of the country. For over two hundred years there were occasional wars between England and Scotland, but the periods of peace were much longer. Then in 1292 Edward I of England was recognized as the overlord of a new Scottish king, John Balliol. Edward tried to use his position to control the Scots. When Balliol refused to obey orders, Edward invaded Scotland. The Scottish king lost his throne, but the Scots resisted grimly, led by William Wallace and later by Robert Bruce.

The famous Declaration of Arbroath expressed the determination of the Scots to be independent:

*'As long as there shall but one hundred of us
remain alive, we will never consent to subject
ourselves to the dominion of the English. For it is
not glory, it is not riches, neither is it honour, but it
is liberty alone that we fight and contend for,
which no honest man will lose but with his life.'*

Robert Bruce became King of Scotland and eventually secured the country's complete independence. But by this time, fighting between English and Scots had become almost a habit. From 1295 Scotland and France fought so often on the same side against the English that their partnership became known to Scots as 'the Auld [old] Alliance'. The Borders – the lands either side of the Anglo-Scots frontier – became a lawless 'Wild West' in which, even in peacetime, there was endless raiding and robbing.

Bruce: Hero or Villain?

When Edward I of England attacked Scotland in 1296, one of his Scottish allies was Robert Bruce (1274–1329), who was a rival of the Scottish king, John Balliol. After English rule was established, Bruce rebelled, but finally submitted to Edward again. Then, in 1306, he murdered John Comyn, a relative of Balliol's. Now a wanted man, Bruce boldly proclaimed himself King of Scotland and led a new rebellion against Edward. Eventually the English were driven from most of Scotland, and in 1314 the Scots won a great victory at Bannockburn. Finally, in 1328, the English were forced to recognize Bruce as king of an independent Scotland.

Robert Bruce ruled Scotland as King Robert I from 1306 to his death in 1329.

This remained the situation even in Tudor times. Prospects for peace looked better in 1503, when Henry VII's elder daughter Margaret married James IV of Scotland. But although a 'perpetual peace' was signed, when England and France went to war in 1512 the Auld Alliance proved as strong as ever. The Scots supported the French, invading England in September 1513. The outcome was to be their greatest-ever disaster, the battle of Flodden, where James IV himself was killed.

In spite of this, the Auld Alliance held firm into the 1540s. In 1542 the Scots were defeated at Solway Moss, and James V died (supposedly of grief) shortly afterwards. His only child was a baby girl, Mary, who became known as Mary, Queen of Scots.

The English king, Henry VIII, now hoped to marry his son Edward to Mary. If the plan had worked, the two kingdoms would have been united. But the Scots rejected the idea, and when an English army captured Edinburgh, the Scots again turned to France for help. The French king sent troops, and Mary was taken to safety in France and engaged to the French king's eldest son.

The Battle of Flodden (1513) was Scotland's greatest military disaster. The Scots invaded Northumberland, but were defeated by the English with the loss of about 10,000 men. The Scottish king, James IV, and many great nobles were among those killed.

By the time Elizabeth I became Queen of England in 1558, Mary had grown up and the situation had become rather different. England was now a firmly Protestant country. Scotland was still garrisoned by French soldiers and ruled by Mary's French mother, who tried to enforce the Catholic religion. But Protestant beliefs and anti-French feeling were growing in Scotland. The Protestants looked to England for help, and in 1560 English troops forced the French to leave Scotland. With Protestants controlling both England and Scotland, the old hatreds became much less important.

In 1560 Mary's husband, Francis II of France, died and she returned to Scotland. There, her position as queen was not easy, since she was a Catholic in a Protestant country. She married a relation, Lord Darnley, and had a son by him, but Darnley's mysterious death and Mary's next marriage (to the Earl of Bothwell) weakened her position even more. Eventually, in 1568, she had to flee from Scotland, leaving her little son James behind.

Mary fled south, into England. But that only created new political problems. England's queen, Elizabeth, was the last surviving child of Henry VIII, and it was becoming clear that she would never marry and have children of her own. If the English crown passed to Elizabeth's nearest relative, that would be Mary, Queen of Scots.

From a Protestant English point of view, the trouble with this was that Mary was a Catholic. With religious hatred at its height over most of Europe, the prospect of a Catholic ruling Protestants seemed terrible. From the moment she arrived, Mary was seen as a danger to Elizabeth and Protestant England. Some English Catholics believed that Elizabeth had no right to the throne (because Henry VIII

Elizabeth I. Most of the Queen's portraits depict her dressed in exotic gowns, covered in jewels and heavily made-up. Elizabeth felt a strong sense of rivalry with Mary, Queen of Scots and both queens are pictured as much younger than their actual ages.

Mary, Queen of Scots [1542–1587]

This portrait of Mary, Queen of Scots was painted after her execution at Fotheringhay Castle in Northamptonshire.

Mary was the daughter of James V of Scotland. She had a claim to the English throne through her grandmother, who was a daughter of Henry VII (see page 10). As a baby she became Queen of Scotland, but to keep her safe from the invading English she was sent to France, where she was married to the boy king Francis II. After Francis's death Mary returned to Scotland, and in 1565 she married her cousin Lord Darnley, who became the father of her son James. Darnley was killed when the house in which he was staying was blown up. It was believed that his murderer was Mary's third husband, the Earl of Bothwell, whom she married in 1567. By marrying Bothwell Mary lost much of her support. She was forced to abdicate in favour of her son, who became James VI of Scotland, and in 1568 she fled to England where she was imprisoned and finally executed. Mary has been seen as a romantic heroine by some – by others as an unscrupulous plotter.

had defied the Pope by marrying her mother), which meant that Mary was the true queen and Elizabeth ought to be removed. Mary's presence in England was bound to encourage ideas of this sort, so when she arrived she was not left free but closely guarded.

Many English Protestants would have been glad to see Mary executed. But Elizabeth was reluctant to sign her death warrant, even when there were Catholic plots to murder Elizabeth and put Mary on the throne. When Mary was found guilty of taking part in one of the plots, Elizabeth still hesitated. Finally, in 1587, after Mary had been in prison for nineteen years, Elizabeth allowed the execution to take place, although she pretended afterwards that it was not what she had intended.

This pretence did help to keep Elizabeth on good terms with Mary's son, who now ruled Scotland as James VI. Brought up as a Protestant, James was Elizabeth's nearest relative. She never named her successor, but when her long reign ended in 1603, her ministers made sure that James became King of England, as James I.

So, after many complications, England and Scotland at last had the same ruler – which was not, however, the same as becoming one country. England had not conquered Scotland or given Scotland a king, as might have been expected; instead, a Scot had become King of England. But in the long run what mattered was that a big step had been taken towards unification.

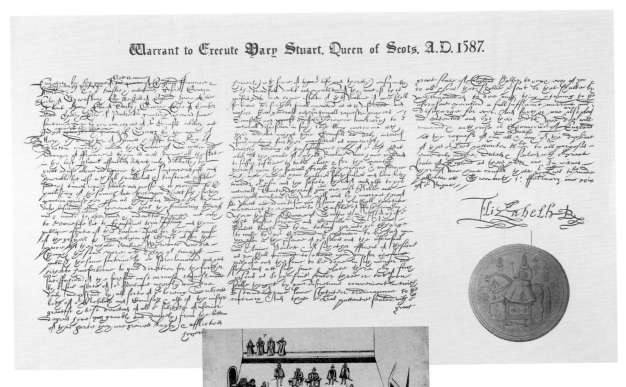

Signed and sealed: the warrant for the execution of Mary, Queen of Scots, issued in the name of Queen Elizabeth.

The execution of Mary, Queen of Scots, at Fotheringhay Castle in February 1587.

5

Upheaval in Ireland

In 1603, for the first time ever, England, Wales, Scotland and Ireland were ruled by the same monarch: James VI of Scotland, who was also James I of England. Prospects for peace in the British Isles must have seemed at their brightest, but in fact a turbulent century lay ahead.

The tensions were most obvious in Ireland, which had been conquered by an English army but remained very different in religion and customs. In Ulster, Hugh O'Neill, Earl of Tyrone, had been forgiven for his rebellion (see page 17), but he was now a servant of the English crown. Because this seemed unbearable, or perhaps because he felt that he was under constant suspicion of disloyalty, he made up his mind to escape. In September 1607, Tyrone, with Rory O'Donnell, Earl of Tyrconnel, and many followers, fled from Ireland by sea.

Hugh O'Neill, Earl of Tyrone, preparing to flee from Ireland. O'Neill may well have believed that his life was in danger if he stayed, but his flight, with many of his followers, meant that there was no-one to oppose James I's policy of 'planting' settlers in Ulster.

The King declared the earls traitors and took over their vast estates in Ulster. To create a group in Ireland that would be loyal to the crown, James took up Elizabeth's plantation policy and applied it on a larger scale. Most of the native Irish landlords in the earls' territories lost their lands, and settlers were brought in from Britain, and especially from Lowland Scotland. The Irish peasants were not driven away, but ownership of the land passed to Protestants. Their numbers gradually increased until they dominated Ulster. This great change influenced the entire history of Ireland, with effects that are still felt today.

Meanwhile in England there were growing conflicts between King and Parliament. Under Charles I (1600–49) these became so serious that the King decided to try and rule without Parliament. During this period (1629–40) his main adviser was Sir Thomas Wentworth, who, as Lord Deputy, ruled Ireland with an iron hand for Charles. But when Charles quarrelled with his Scottish subjects, he was forced to call Parliament and submit to its demands – one of which was for Wentworth's head. This Parliament – later known as the Long Parliament – began to introduce important political and religious changes.

In 1641, Irish Catholics rose in revolt. They were afraid of what the anti-Catholic Long Parliament might do to them, and they resented the Ulster plantations. The revolt blazed up first in the north of Ireland, where many Protestant settlers were massacred. The effect on English politics was disastrous. Exaggerated reports of the bloodshed in Ireland caused outcry and a fury of anti-Irish and anti-Catholic feeling in England.

Worse was to come. An English army had to be raised to crush the Irish rebellion. Parliament was prepared to pay for an army, but was afraid to let the King lead it: when the army had done its job, Charles might turn it on Parliament. Yet the King was the traditional commander-in-chief, and could not possibly let Parliament control the army. No agreement could be reached, and, more than any other issue, this caused Charles and his Parliament to take up arms against each other. If there had not been an Irish rebellion in 1641, it is at least possible that there would have been no English Civil War.

Thomas Wentworth, Earl of Strafford (1593–1641) ruled Ireland as Lord Deputy from 1632–39. Charles I recalled him to England where he became the king's chief advisor. MPs serving in the Long Parliament demanded his execution and he was beheaded in 1641.

Protest. Rebel

Ireland

The capture of a town in Ireland during the rebellion in 1641.

Oliver Cromwell, victorious general in the Parliamentary army and later Lord Protector of the Commonwealth.

Parliament won the Civil War (1642–45), and Charles I was finally executed in January 1649. England became a republic known as the Commonwealth. The new government sent its outstanding general, Oliver Cromwell (1599–1658), to reconquer Ireland from the royalists and Catholics, and to revenge the massacres of 1641. At the siege of Drogheda, and later at Wexford, Cromwell ordered that none of the defenders should be spared. He wrote of the action at Drogheda that:

'I think that night they put to the sword about 2,000 men. I am persuaded that this is a righteous judgement of God upon these barbarous wretches, and that it will tend to prevent the spilling of blood for the future.'

These massacres, and the punishing new policy that followed, were never forgotten by the Catholic Irish. Ireland's parliament was abolished. The many Irish landlords whose loyalty was in doubt lost their lands or were pushed out into remote Connaught, in the far west of Ireland. Parliamentary soldiers and other settlers replaced the landlords in the rest of Ireland. The Catholic peasants remained

28

where they were, but the landowning class became over-whelmingly Protestant. In the seventeenth century it was the landowners who mattered, so a Protestant minority now dominated Ireland.

After a few years the Commonwealth collapsed, and in 1660 Charles I's son returned from exile to become king as Charles II. The Irish parliament was restored and some roy-alists recovered their lands, but most of Cromwell's harsh arrangements remained unchanged. Charles told his Irish Catholic subjects with brutal frankness, 'My justice I must afford to you all, but my favour must be given to my Protestant subjects.' For most of the time Catholics were tolerated under Charles II, but that was all.

The situation changed completely when Charles's Catholic brother, James II, became king. In England, James (1685–88) promoted his fellow-Catholics and tried to do away with the laws that had been passed against them. He put the Catholic Earl of Tyrconnel in charge of Ireland with instructions to follow a similar policy. But then James was overthrown by the 'Glorious Revolution' of 1688, and the Protestants William of Orange (William III, 1650–1702) and Mary were installed as joint monarchs.

The Siege of Londonderry (1689), seen from the walls of the city. Londonderry and Enniskillen were the only towns to hold out when Catholic Ireland rose in support of James II. The heroic 105-day defence of Londonderry is still celebrated by Northern Irish Protestants.

The Catholic Irish naturally continued to support the exiled James. But although James landed in Ireland, backed by French troops, he was defeated by William's forces. In 1691 the last of his followers surrendered at Limerick. William III agreed that Irish Catholics should be tolerated as they had been under Charles II, but when the Protestant-dominated Irish Parliament met, it refused to carry out the agreement. New laws were passed to make sure that Catholics remained powerless and poor. No Catholic could sit in Parliament, hold government office, or become a lawyer. Educational opportunities for Catholics were limited. Above all, it became impossible for the remaining Catholic landowners to enlarge their possessions, and hard for them even to keep the lands they still held. By 1700 the 'Old English' lords and Irish chiefs had been replaced by a new Protestant ruling class, loyal to the crown and dependent on it. Brutally but effectively, English rule in Ireland had been made secure.

William's Irish War

In March 1689 the exiled James II landed at Kinsale, hoping to use Ireland as a base and recover his entire kingdom. His Catholic followers, backed by French troops, soon controlled most of the island. James's forces besieged the city of Londonderry, where the (Protestant) apprentice boys became famous for their quick response in closing the gates against James. The siege lasted for 105 days until help arrived. In the following year, 1690, William III landed with an army and defeated James at the Battle of the Boyne, a river just north of Dublin. James fled to France, but his followers fought on for another year before surrendering. In present-day Northern Ireland, which is still bitterly divided, Protestants continue to celebrate the Siege of Londonderry and the Battle of the Boyne.

William III leads his troops at the Battle of the Boyne (1690). His victory ended James II's hopes of winning back his kingdom, using Ireland as a base.

6

The Islands United?

In 1603 James VI of Scotland became James I of England (see page 24). But Scotland and England remained separate countries. Scotland kept its own parliament, and also its own form of Protestant Church, which had developed in a different way from England's.

But having the same king did make a difference to relations between the two countries. Once the Borders were firmly policed on both sides, lawlessness in the area was stamped out. In other ways the king's policy carried the two

James VI of Scotland (1566–1625). In 1603 he inherited the throne of England, where he was known as James I. His plans to unite England and Scotland succeeded but only long after his death.

countries along together, so that they would, for example, normally fight on the same side in a war. James was keen to go further and persuade Scots and English to unite into a single country. He tried to make them feel closer by calling himself King of 'Great Britain', a term that was eventually accepted to describe England, Wales and Scotland. A flag was even designed which combined the English cross of St George and the Scottish cross of St Andrew. But James's proposals for a full union were scorned by the English Parliament, despite his powerful arguments:

> 'Hath he (God) not made us all in one island, compassed with one sea and of itself by nature indivisible? And now in the end and fulness of time he hath untied the right and title of both kingdoms ... whereby it is now become like a little world within itself, being intrenched and fortified round about with a natural and yet admirable strong pond or ditch. What God hath conjoined let no man separate.'

As long as the Scots and English obeyed the King, the separation between the countries did not matter much. But that changed when Charles I tried to force his religious ideas on the Scots (1637). They rebelled, and defeated the army Charles led against them. All the King's plans were

Charles I's strongly-held belief in his 'god-given' right to rule and his desire to force his own form of Protestantism on his subjects caused deep divisions among the people.

An English cartoon printed in 1638, showing a Scot handing a petition to Charles I asking him to change his religious policy in Scotland. Charles's refusal led to ruinous civil wars.

ruined, since the cost of the fighting meant that he had to call the English Parliament and ask it for money. For eleven years he had ruled without Parliament, so when the new Long Parliament met in 1640, MPs voted to limit Charles's power before allowing him any new grants of money.

The Scottish Highlands

There were two very different ways of life in Scotland. In the Lowlands of the south and east, people lived settled lives and spoke English. The Highlanders of the north and north-west still spoke the ancient Scots tongue, Gaelic. They belonged to a warrior society made up of clans such as the Macdonalds, Camerons and Macleods. Clans were like huge families, each of them completely loyal to the clan chief and often at war with their neighbours. To Lowlanders and the government in London, the Highlanders seemed like barbarians, always feuding, cattle-raiding or rebelling. But their reckless courage, and their skill with the claymore (sword) and dirk (dagger), made them fearsome and respected fighters.

The wild and rugged Scottish Highlands – home of the warrior clans. Life for the Highland clansmen was very different from that of the Scots living in the Lowlands.

Charles was forced to agree, but relations between the King and Parliament became more and more strained. As we saw in the last chapter, the Catholic revolt in Charles's third kingdom, Ireland, made it certain that the quarrel would turn into a civil war.

Over the next few years the Scots behaved with great independence. In 1643 they entered the English Civil War on the side of Parliament. At the end of the war, with Parliament victorious, Charles surrendered to the Scots, hoping to get better terms from them; but in 1647 they sold him to the English parliamentarians.

However, the Scots soon became disillusioned with their English allies, and after Charles I's execution in 1649 they recognized his exiled son as King Charles II. But the Scottish army proved no match for the Commonwealth's New Model Army led by Oliver Cromwell, who had just returned from his bloody conquests in Ireland. In 1650–51 he won decisive victories at the battles of Dunbar and Worcester, and Scotland was occupied by his troops. The Scots Parliament, like Ireland's, was abolished. A single government, soon led by Cromwell himself as Lord Protector, ruled the British Isles.

Oliver Cromwell at the Battle of Dunbar, 1650. After defeating both the Scots and the Irish, Cromwell briefly united the British Isles by force.

This was a full union, but it was based entirely on force. The Scots sent MPs to the Parliament at Westminster, but real power rested with Cromwell and the parliamentary army. After his death the Commonwealth fell apart, Charles II was restored, and England, Scotland and Ireland became separate kingdoms again.

The Scots were glad about this, but they realized that there had been some important advantages in their brief union with England. Under Cromwell the Scots had been able to trade freely with England and the English colonies overseas. For a small, poor but energetic people like the Scots, this opened up exciting new opportunities and prospects of wealth. The opportunities disappeared once their country became independent again. As a result the idea of an Anglo-Scottish union became more attractive, and discussions about it were held as early as the 1670s. For the time being, however, no agreement was reached.

William III and Mary were joint rulers of England and Scotland from 1688 to 1694. Then the Dutch-born William ruled alone until his death in 1702.

The Massacre of Glencoe

The Macdonalds were one of the Highland clans that rebelled against William and Mary in 1689. They were told they would be forgiven if they took an oath of loyalty to the new monarchs. Their chief took the oath, but later than he should have done. Using the excuse that the Macdonalds were now outlaws, one of King William's ministers, the Earl of Stair, ordered that they should be killed. English troops and members of the rival Campbell clan, who had been staying with the Macdonalds at Glencoe, suddenly turned on them without warning and slaughtered thirty-eight of the clan. The Earl of Stair had wanted to teach the unruly Highlanders a lesson, but the massacre caused a scandal which ruined his career.

Clansmen fleeing after the infamous Massacre of Glencoe.

Later, the separate existence of England and Scotland caused new difficulties. In 1688 the Catholic King James II (James VII of Scotland) was replaced in England by William and Mary (see page 29).

Scotland accepted the new rulers, although followers of James – known as the Jacobites – resisted for a time with the help of some Highland clans. But during the reigns of William and Mary (and later William III on his own), Parliament played a larger role in both England and Scotland – but the two parliaments and peoples sometimes pulled in different directions.

The key moment for the Scots was the failure of the Darien scheme. In 1695, unable to trade freely with England and its colonies, the Scots decided to compete with England by founding a colony of their own. They hoped that trade based at Darien, on the isthmus of Panama (Central America), would make Scotland a great economic power. Instead, the failure of the colony almost ruined the country.

Scots blamed England, which had certainly not been helpful. But the episode showed that, on its own, Scotland lacked the resources to become strong and wealthy in the wider world.

Fortunately a political crisis persuaded the English that a union with Scotland would be a good idea. Queen Anne came to the throne in England and Scotland in 1702, but she had no surviving children. When she died, the Scots would be free to choose their own monarch – and if they chose differently from the English, Scotland would again be truly independent and a threat to England. This seemed particularly important since England was engaged in a long, exhausting war against France. A union that made England and Scotland a single country would solve the problem once and for all.

Queen Anne (1665–1714), the younger daughter of James II. She died childless and the English government feared a political crisis after her death. This fear, and other concerns, encouraged the English to seek a more binding union with the Scots.

Since the English government was eager for agreement, the Scots were able to get good terms. The first article of the Act of Union laid down that 'The Two Kingdoms of England and Scotland shall for ever after be united into one Kingdom by the name of Great Britain.' There was to be a single parliament at Westminster, to which the Scots would send 45 MPs and 16 Lords. Scotland's legal system and Church would not be changed. Special arrangements would help the Scots to fit in with England's financial system. And all subjects of the crown would have 'full freedom and intercourse of trade and navigation to and from any port or place within the said United Kingdom and the dominions and plantations thereunto belonging'.

On 16 January 1707 the Scottish Parliament passed the Act of Union and ceased to exist. The Scottish Chancellor remarked 'Now there's an end to ane auld sang' – the 'old song' being the long, romantic history of an independent Scotland. But he signed the Act, and James I's hope for a united Great Britain (see page 33) was finally realized.

Queen Anne receiving the Treaty of Union (1707), which merged England, Wales and Scotland into a single country known as Great Britain. The Union gave England political security, while Scotland could now trade freely with England and its colonies.

7

A Look Ahead

King George I of Great Britain. This German king spoke no English, but he fitted in with the developing British political system, which brought a new stability.

After the Act of Union the war against France was brought to an end in 1713. A year later, when Queen Anne died, her nearest Protestant relative, the Elector (ruler) of Hanover in Germany, became King George I (1714–27). After this, British kings and queens followed one another in smooth succession. England, Wales and Scotland had become a single nation, and Ireland, although still in theory a separate kingdom, was also run from London. By 1750 Britain had become a great power.

So, in a very important sense, unification had worked. As a single nation, the kingdom was no longer threatened by quarrels between its peoples. It was also safer from its enemies overseas. And unification meant that Britain had a larger workforce and greater resources with which to trade, make war, colonize and build up an empire. In the new British state England had the biggest population and the most wealth, but the other nations made a very large contribution. To take examples from two very different occupations, many of the finest writers and the most famous army regiments have come from Wales, Scotland and Ireland.

However, there were alarms in the years following the union between England and Scotland. The economic benefits took longer to arrive than many Scots had expected, and in 1713 a proposal to end the union was only defeated in the House of Lords by four votes. But a more serious threat came from the Highlands, where some clans supported the exiled Stuart descendants of James II. These supporters were called Jacobites (Jacobus is Latin for James). A rebellion in 1715, led by James II's son, the 'Old Pretender' (claimant), was put down quite easily, but in 1745 his son Charles ('Bonnie Prince Charlie' or the Young Pretender) led a more dangerous uprising. The Prince promised to restore a separate kingdom of Scotland, but

The Battle of Prestonpans, where the Highlanders, led by Prince Charles Edward Stuart, defeated British troops in 1745.

The Jacobite Rebellion of 1745

In July 1745 Prince Charles Edward Stuart landed in Scotland, hoping to recover the throne for the exiled Stuarts. The Prince, popularly known as Bonnie Prince Charlie, raised his standard at Glenfinnan in the Highlands and proclaimed his father James III, King of England and Scotland. Joined by many of the Highland clans, he occupied Edinburgh, defeated an English army at Prestonpans, and marched south. But to his disappointment there was little support for him in England. At Derby, with enemy armies closing in, he was forced to turn back. After a last victory at Falkirk, the Highlanders were crushed at the Battle of Culloden in April 1746. After many adventures, the Prince escaped from Scotland.

Charles Edward Stuart, often called 'Bonnie Prince Charlie'.

(right) A memorial on Culloden Moor set up to commemorate the Highlanders who were slaughtered at the Battle of Culloden in 1746.

THE BATTLE OF CULLODEN WAS FOUGHT ON THIS MOOR 16TH APRIL 1746. THE GRAVES OF THE GALLANT HIGHLANDERS WHO FOUGHT FOR SCOTLAND & PRINCE CHARLIE ARE MARKED BY THE NAMES OF THEIR CLANS

The Battle of Culloden. In the background and right foreground Highlanders can be seen charging into a volley of musket-fire from tightly-formed ranks of English troops.

the Lowlanders still refused to support him. After Charles had been defeated, the Highlanders were savagely punished and the Highland way of life was destroyed.

Unification helped to make Britain powerful and wealthy, so it can easily be seen as a success story. But for a very long time the change mainly benefited the rich and powerful in the countries concerned. Many talented people in Wales, Scotland and Ireland were drawn away from home to make careers in England, and especially London. The old cultures suffered, and the native languages came close to dying out. Nobody can really say what would have happened if unification had not taken place, but it is worth remembering that all changes involve losses as well as gains. And we must not think that, because something happened, it was necessarily 'all for the best'.

It is certainly hard to believe this in the case of Ireland. There, the injustices done to the Catholic majority made it likely that there would be trouble sooner or later. But it proved to be later – well after 1750. There is only space enough here to note that an Act of Union in 1801 did finally join Britain and Ireland in a new state named the United Kingdom. But the union did nothing to alter the basic situation, and the relationship between Britain and Ireland continued to be an unhappy one.

Unification made the peoples of the British Isles more alike in their way of life – in their work, in their interests and through their shared use of the English language. In more recent times, radio, television and newspapers, putting over the same images and ideas to everybody, have emphasized this alikeness. Yet national traditions and symbols are still treasured, and the different peoples of the islands still think of themselves as distinct communities. If, as some people believe, the day of the strong, centralized state is coming to an end, the survival of national differences may yet prove to be important.

Slogans and symbols on a wall at Larne in Northern Ireland. The references to William III and the Battle of the Boyne, fought in 1690, show how strongly past events still influence present-day Northern Irish attitudes.

None of this could be foreseen in 1750, of course. What mattered then was the emergence of a united Great Britain as a powerful, confident and unified state, that was about to become a great imperial power and the world's first industrial nation.

The Houses of Parliament at Westminster. Although once a village outside London, Westminster is now part of the capital and the term is often used to mean the British government. 'Westminster' is the supreme authority for the entire United Kingdom – England, Scotland, Wales and Northern Ireland.

Time Line

1500–1550

◊ **1485** Battle of Bosworth; Henry VII becomes King of England

◊ **1503** Henry's daughter Margaret marries James IV of Scotland

◊ **1509** Henry VIII comes to the throne

◊ **1513** Scots invade England, are beaten at Battle of Flodden

◊ **1534** Revolt led by Kildare in Ireland defeated

◊ **1536** Union of England and Wales

◊ **1541** Henry VIII takes title King of Ireland

◊ **1544** English capture Leith and Edinburgh

◊ **1547** Mary, Queen of Scots sent to France

| 1500 | 1510 | 1520 | 1530 | 1540 | 1550 |

1550–1600

◊ **1558** Elizabeth I becomes Queen of England

◊ **1560** Mary, Queen of Scots returns to Scotland

◊ **1568** Mary, Queen of Scots flees to England, is imprisoned

◊ **1579** Irish revolt led by James FitzMaurice, Earl of Desmond

◊ **1583** Desmond defeated; Munster laid waste; first Irish plantations

◊ **1587** Execution of Mary, Queen of Scots

◊ **1594** Rebellions in Ireland led by Hugh O'Neill, Earl of Tyrone

◊ **1598** English force in Ireland defeated at Yellow Ford; Earl of Essex sent to subdue Irish rebellion

| 1550 | 1560 | 1570 | 1580 | 1590 | 1600 |

1600–1650

◊ **1600** Lord Mountjoy replaces Essex

◊ **1603** Mountjoy defeats Irish rebels; James VI of Scotland becomes James I of England

◊ **1607** Flight of Tyrone and other Irish earls; Union of England and Scotland rejected by English Parliament

◊ **1608** English and Scottish settlers in Ulster

◊ **1625** Charles I becomes King of England and Scotland

◊ **1641** Irish rebellion

◊ **1642–46** English Civil War

◊ **1648** Scots defeated at Preston

◊ **1649** Charles I executed; massacres in Ireland

| 1600 | 1610 | 1620 | 1630 | 1640 | 1650 |

1650–1700

◊ **1650** Cromwell invades Scotland, defeats Scots at Dunbar

◊ **1652** Cromwellian settlement of Ireland

◊ **1660** Charles II restored

◊ **1662** Act of Settlement in Ireland

◊ **1685** James II succeeds to throne

◊ **1688** William and Mary offered throne; flight of James II

◊ **1689** James lands in Ireland; Siege of Londonderry; Rebellion in Scotland

◊ **1690** James II beaten by William III at Battle of the Boyne

◊ **1691** Treaty of Limerick ends revolt in Ireland

◊ **1692** Massacre of Glencoe

◊ **1695** Failure of Darien scheme

| 1650 | 1660 | 1670 | 1680 | 1690 | 1700 |

1700–1750

◊ **1702** Anne succeeds to throne

◊ **1707** Act of Union unites Scotland, England and Wales

◊ **1714** George I becomes King

◊ **1715** Jacobite rebellion in north, defeated at Preston

◊ **1727** George II succeeds to throne

◊ **1745** Second Jacobite rebellion

◊ **1746** Final defeat of Jacobites at Battle of Culloden

◊ **1801** Act of Union creates the United Kingdom

| 1700 | 1710 | 1720 | 1730 | 1740 | 1750 |

Glossary

Abdicate To give up the throne.

Alliance An agreement between people or nations (allies) who work together.

Barbarous Savage or uncivilized.

Campaign Military operations in a war area.

Celts Inhabitants of Britain and Ireland before the Anglo-Saxon invasions.

Clans Small groups or tribes.

Colonization The sending of settlers to establish a settlement or colony.

Commonwealth The republic that existed in Britain from 1649 to 1660.

Disunited Lacking in unity – describes a group of people who are quarrelling among themselves.

Exile Being unable to return to one's own country.

Garrison Troops more or less permanently based in a particular place, usually in order to guard it.

Glorious Revolution The ousting of James II and establishment of William III and his wife Mary on the English throne.

Guerrilla warfare Fighting involving the use of ambushes and traps, often used when fighting stronger forces.

Imperial Referring to an empire.

Isthmus A narrow neck of land connecting two larger land areas.

Marcher lords Lords who governed and defended the Welsh Marches, the border lands between Wales and England.

Massacre The brutal murder of large numbers of people.

Musket A long-barrelled gun which was carried by foot solders.

National symbol An object that stands for a country – for example the rose for England and the thistle for Scotland.

Patron saint The saint who is especially connected with a country and is believed to act as its protector – for example St Patrick is the patron saint of Ireland.

Picts A people who lived in what is now Scotland, before the Scots arrived.

Pike A weapon, similar to a long spear, carried by foot soldiers.

Plantation An organized settlement of newcomers 'planted' or set up in another country.

Reformation The religious movement in sixteenth-century Europe, which began as an attempt to reform the Roman Catholic Church and resulted in the establishment of Protestant churches.

Resources Money, materials or manpower, available for use by a country or government.

Royalists Supporters of Charles I during the English Civil War, and of the Crown at other times.

Terrain The nature of the ground (flat or hilly, boggy or dry, etc.) especially from a military point of view.

Toleration Permitting people to hold different ideas and beliefs.

Treaties Formal agreements or contracts between states.

Unified To have become one, united.

Books to Read

Robert Bruce by Margaret Stephen (Wayland, 1995)
Owain Glyndŵr by Glanmore Williams (University of Wales Press, 1993)
The Jacobites by Iain Rose (Wayland, 1995)
James VI/I by Kaye Kallonatis (Wayland, 1995)
The Making of the United Kingdom by Joe Scott (Heinemann, 1993)
Tudor Monarchs by Jessica Sarrauga (Batsford, 1992)

The Union of 1707 by Iain Rose (Wayland, 1996)
A Wider World – The Making of the United Kingdom by Rosemary Kelly (Stanley Thorne, 1992)

For older readers
Conquest and Union: Fashioning a British State ed. by Steven G. Ellis and Sarah Barber (Longman, 1995)

Places of Interest to Visit

Caernarfon Castle, Caernarfon, North Wales.
One of the many splendid Norman castles built by King Edward I in Wales. Caernarfon Castle is traditionally the site of the investiture of the eldest son of the monarch as Prince of Wales. Other interesting Welsh castles to visit are at Pembroke, Conwy, Harlech and Beaumaris in Anglesey.

National Museum of Wales, Cardiff.
Permanent collections illustrate the story of Wales from earliest times.

The Castle, Edinburgh.
This famous landmark has brooded over Scotland's capital for centuries.

Palace of Holyroodhouse, Royal Mile, Edinburgh.
The palace was first built in 1500. It is the official residence of the Queen in Scotland. Visitors can see the Throne Room and the State Apartments of Charles II and Mary, Queen of Scots.

Houses of Parliament, Westminster, London.
It may be possible to visit the Houses of Parliament when the government is not in session. You can find out by contacting your local MP.

Public Record Office Museum, Chancery Lane, London.
The museum contains a permanent exhibition of

manuscripts and archives of national importance, illustrating many well-known episodes in British history.

Windsor Castle, Windsor, Berkshire.
The castle has been a royal residence since 1110. Visitors can see the State Apartments which contain valuable collections of furniture, paintings and portraits.

National Museum of Ireland, 7–9 Merrion Row, Dublin, Ireland.
The historical section of the museum illustrates the political history of Ireland from 1700 until the achievement of independence.

Index